WEEKLY WR READER®
EARLY LEARNING LIBRARY

Let's Read About Weather

Let's Read About

Wind

by Kristin Boerger

**Reading Consultant: Susan Nations, M.Ed.,
author/literacy coach/consultant
in literacy development**

Please visit our web site at: www.garethstevens.com
For a free color catalog describing Weekly Reader® Early Learning Library's list
of high-quality books, call 1-877-445-5824 (USA) or 1-800-387-3178 (Canada).
Weekly Reader® Early Learning Library's fax: (414) 336-0164.

Library of Congress Cataloging-in-Publication Data

Boerger, Kristin.
    Let's read about wind / by Kristin Boerger.
       p. cm. — (Let's read about weather)
    ISBN-13: 978-0-8368-7808-0 (lib. bdg.)
    ISBN-13: 978-0-8368-7813-4 (softcover)
    1. Winds—Juvenile literature.   I. Title.
  QC931.4.B64   2006
  551.51'8—dc22   2006029352

This edition first published in 2007 by
Weekly Reader® Early Learning Library
A Member of the WRC Media Family of Companies
330 West Olive Street, Suite 100
Milwaukee, WI 53212 USA

Editor: Dorothy L. Gibbs
Art direction: Tammy West
Cover design and page layout: Dave Kowalski
Photo research: Diane Laska-Swanke

Picture credits: Cover, title, © David Young-Wolff/PhotoEdit; pp. 4, 12 (upper right) © Myrleen Ferguson Cate/
PhotoEdit; pp. 5, 12 (lower right) © Jeff Greenberg/PhotoEdit; pp. 6, 7 Gregg Andersen; p. 8 © Tony Freeman/
PhotoEdit; pp. 9, 12 (lower left) © Lynwood M. Chace/Photo Researchers, Inc.; pp. 10, 11, 12 (upper left)
Courtesy of Joy Manners-Astley

Printed in the United States of America

1 2 3 4 5 6 7 8 9 10 10 09 08 07 06

Note to Educators and Parents

Learning to read is one of the most exciting and challenging things young children do. Among other skills, they are beginning to match the spoken word to print and learn directionality and print conventions. Books that are appropriate for emergent readers will incorporate many of these conventions while also being appealing and entertaining.

The books in the *Let's Read About Weather* series are designed to support young readers in the earliest stages of literacy. They will love looking at the full-color photographs while learning about the exciting variety of weather. Each book will invite children to read — and reread — again and again!

In addition to serving as wonderful picture books in schools, libraries, and homes, this series is specifically intended to be read within instructional small groups. The small group setting enables the teacher or other adult to provide scaffolding that will boost the reader's efforts. Children and adults alike will find these books supportive, engaging, and fun!

> — Susan Nations, M.Ed., author/literacy coach/
> consultant in literacy development

Wind blows the kite.

Wind blows the tree.

Wind blows
the hat

away from me!

Wind blows
the boat.

Wind blows
the seeds.

9

Wind blows
the bubbles

away from me!

Glossary

bubbles

kite

seeds

tree

away from me!

Glossary

bubbles	kite
seeds	tree